Reflections

of WIRRAL

New images of the
Wirral Peninsula

GUY HUNTINGTON and
KENNETH BURNLEY

Mill Hill
Publishing
Limited

Published by Mill Hill Publishing Ltd, Wirral, CH61 4XU
www.millhillpublishing.co.uk
Email: enquiries@millhillpublishing.co.uk

First published 2011

British Library Cataloguing-in-Publication Data
A catalogue record for this book is available from the British Library.

ISBN: 978-0-9557724-1-2

Title page photo: Sailing on the Marine Lake, West Kirby
Page 4 photo: Thornton Hough

Designed and typeset by Kenneth Burnley, Wirral, Cheshire
Printed and bound in England by Butler Tanner & Dennis Ltd, Frome, Somerset

Contents

Introduction

The Wirral Peninsula has always been a special place, 'a place apart'. Perhaps it's because it is surrounded on three sides by water – to the north, the Irish Sea; to the east, the River Mersey; and to the west, the River Dee. Historically part of Cheshire, and with its southern border reaching almost up to the city of Chester, its inhabitants are fiercely proud and protective of its unique and special identity that doesn't really put it into any of the surrounding territories.

From its higher ground one can see many kingdoms and counties. To the west, the high hills of Wales, with Flintshire county wetting its toes in the Dee waters, and the Snowdonia peaks a fitting backcloth, or the Ormesheads jutting out into the sea. To the north, the coastline of Lancashire fading northwards to the Cumbrian fells and the Scottish hills of Galloway, with, if the day is exceptionally clear, a glimpse of the Isle of Man. To the east, the tops of the taller Liverpool buildings, and behind them the Pennine chain with Winter Hill prominent in the haze. And to the south, indistinct outlines of woods and low hills, maybe the top of Chester Cathedral; and beyond, many miles of historic borderlands, marcher territory, rich in history.

Yet Wirral has tended to ally itself with none of those bigger expanses. Yes, both Liverpool and Chester have each had some influence over the peninsula: much of what we see here today owes its existence to the two neighbouring cities. But its address is not 'Wirral, Liverpool' or 'Wirral, Chester'. Today it's just 'WIRRAL' followed by its CH postcode. So it is a place in its own right, not a subservient entity. When asked 'Where do you live?', we reply 'Oh, The Wirral', as if the questioner should know exactly where it is. And if they don't, we then say something like 'It's the peninsula sandwiched between Wales and Liverpool, just north of Chester.' And woe betide anyone who says it's a suburb of Liverpool, or Chester!

That's *where* it is; but *what* is the Wirral Peninsula? This book has the answer, in words and pictures. It leads you on a richly coloured and textured tour of its countryside and coast, its towns, villages and buildings. Two decades ago the authors portrayed Wirral through *Images of Wirral*, a book that was well received and widely acclaimed by both residents and visitors. In this new book, they revisit the peninsula and, through the use of camera and pen, proudly exhibit the place in a new and refreshing way that is sure to delight and please all who pick up the book. Modern descriptions are interspersed with accounts from visitors of the past, to add an element of nostalgia to what has always been – and will be – a place of constant change.

So pick up this book in the knowledge that the unique 'something' that makes Wirral such a special place has been garnered here within these pages – and having read, and marvelled, go out and explore these and all the other nooks and crannies that make up this very special corner of England!

SEA
REFLECTIONS

'West Kirby is delightfully situated at the entrance to the River Dee, with Liverpool Bay on one side, the broad expanse of the Irish Sea in front, and at the back, undulating hills covered with ferns and purple heather. It is here that the ever-restless sea is seen in all its varied moods: at times like unto a sheet of glass, reflecting the fleecy cloud and the azure blue, or the bright rays of the sun, in crimson glare or amber light.'

JOHN THOMPSON, 1894

Sunset over Hilbre.

West Kirby, Hilbre and Hoylake

Driving north along the high road from Chester, there comes a point where the quality of the sky changes from 'inland light' to 'coastal light'. It's hard to describe if you've never noticed it, but most Wirral folk know about it. It's more noticeable later in the day, and in the spring, summer and autumn, for then the sun is shining on the sea, and its reflection is bounced back into the skies above Wirral. This is one of the many things that make the Wirral Peninsula so special.

The sea laps Wirral from the Dee Estuary in the west along a seven-mile coastline to the Mersey Estuary in the east. It swirls around the sandstone cliffs of the Hilbre Isles at high tide, and creeps relentlessly across the wide, sandy expanses of the Dee Estuary from the tip of Wirral to the tip of Wales.

From Hoylake to Meols a rail-guarded, house-lined promenade gives both walker and driver a fine view northwards (note that, were it not for the Isle of Man, the next land-mass northwards from here is Iceland!). Beyond Meols, and all the way to Harrison Drive, a strong, sloping embankment keeps the Irish Sea from inundating the low-lying land of north Wirral. Landward, the grassy meadows are lovely in summer with seaside plants and butterflies. At Leasowe Bay, the crescent of remnant sandhills fronts a wide, sandy beach, a favourite place for paddlers and swimmers.

Wirral's north coast ends at New Brighton, the old cliffline preserved by the promenade, before the peninsula turns sharply south down the Mersey.

OPPOSITE
West Kirby and Hoylake from the air. In the foreground, West Kirby sits quietly beside the Marine Lake at low tide. At the top lies Hoylake, and towards the left, the links of the Royal Liverpool Golf Club and the tip of Red Rocks.

BELOW
West Kirby from Caldy Hill. In the foreground, the greening birches of spring. Beyond the town, the Marine Lake, Hilbre Island and the Dee Estuary.

LEFT
The Mariners' Beacon rises above West Kirby as a prominent landmark seen from miles around. The windmill that had formerly stood on this hill was used as a mark for shipping and, when it was blown down, the Liverpool Docks Trustees replaced it with the present beacon. It reads 'This column was erected by the Trustees of the Liverpool Docks, by permission of John Shaw Leigh, Esq., owner of the land, who also granted the stone for its erection, Anno Domini 1841, as a Beacon for mariners frequenting the River Mersey and its vicinity. The foundation stone was laid April 16th 1841 by John Shaw Leigh Esquire'.

RIGHT
The Grade II listed War Memorial on Grange Hill was designed by the renowned war sculptor Charles Jagger and unveiled on 16 December 1922.

St Bridget's Parish Church, West Kirby, probably one of the earliest Christian sites in Cheshire. Home of the wonderful ancient hogback stone, and adjacent to the Charles Dawson Brown Museum, a treasure-house of sculptured and carved stones.

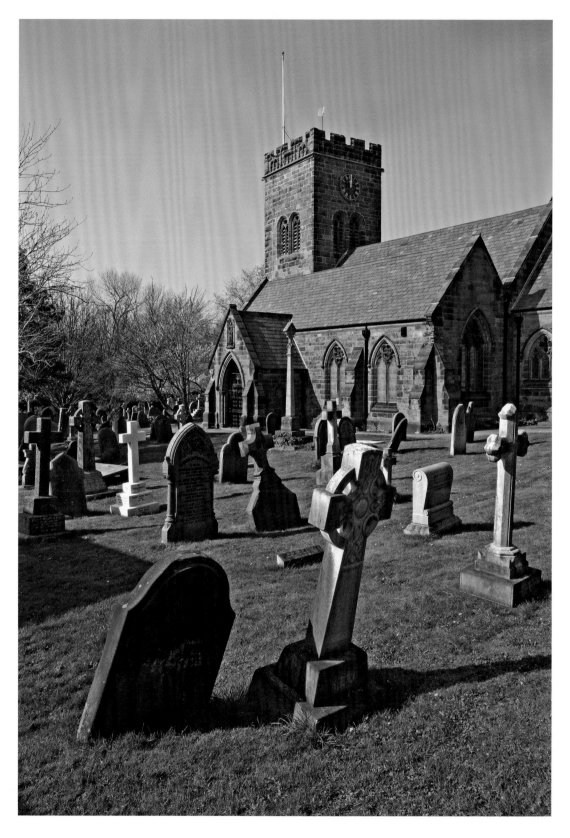

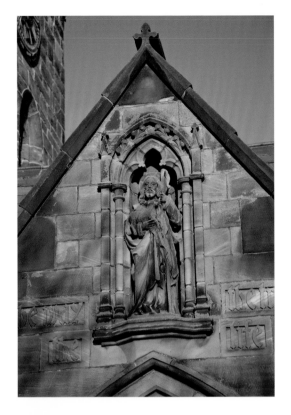

ABOVE LEFT
Sculptured stone detail from
St Bridget's Church.

ABOVE RIGHT
The lychgate, St Bridget's
Church.

LEFT
Attractive town houses in
Banks Road, West Kirby.

PAGES 14–15
Moonrise over
the Marine Lake,
West Kirby.

ABOVE
The promenade and
Marine Lake.

BELOW
Red-breasted Merganser
on the Marine Lake.

PAGE 18 (TOP)
Stormy skies over
Hilbre.

PAGE 18 (BOTTOM)
A flock of Knot flying
over the Marine Lake.

PAGE 19
Hilbre Island from
the air.

The Marine Lake, West Kirby, with the Welsh hills in the distance. The original lake was opened in 1899 and expanded in modern times. 'If you have not visited West Kirby for 30 years, you will find that what you left a village has now grown into a little town, with a parade, in front of which has been constructed a large salt-water lake on the seashore, on which are pleasure-boats; so that at the lowest ebb, the artificial lake gives the visitor the feeling that he is resting by the sea.' (H. E. Young, *A Perambulation of the Hundred of Wirral*, 1909)

BELOW
Sailing boats preparing for the annual Wilson Trophy event on the Marine Lake.

17

The estuary and its wet sands attract thousands of waders, especially during autumn, winter and spring. Here, a flock of Sanderling and Dunlin soars above the sands.

A winter's day on the Dee Estuary: Hilbre Island backed by the snow-clad heights of the distant Welsh Carneddau.

A pair of Redshank
resting on rocks near
the Marine Lake, West
KIrby.

OPPOSITE
Sandstone features of Hilbre include this natural arch (top) and the 'Lady's Cave', where, legend has it, a love-struck maiden was washed up, and died, brokenhearted, in the arms of a monk.

BELOW
The few buildings on Hilbre include private cottages and the bird observatory.

'Finally, you must cross to Hilbre with me. You will have noticed the three sandstone islands from either Hoylake or West Kirby, rather more than a mile from the shore. On a warm summer day, there is no better spot for a family picnic. In the rockpools may be found shrimps, gobies, starfish and crabs of all sorts; the botanist will want to investigate the seaweeds; the fisherman will find sport from the old lifeboat slip at the north end of Hilbre; the ordinary person will find it a delightful way of passing a lazy, carefree day in the open air and sunshine. At low tide, the seals sunbathe on the big sandbank west of Hilbre: I have counted more than 200 there at the one time and watched them through my glasses rolling over on their fat backs, stretching and scratching themselves in pure enjoyment.

But to bird lovers, the real Hilbre is to be found between September and April, when the birds assemble there in countless thousands. It is doubtful if any other area around our coast can better it for waders, both in number and variety.'

(*Hoylake and West Kirby Guide*, undated)

Between West Kirby and the northwesterly tip of Wirral lies the Red Rocks SSSI, a mile-long stretch of sandy beach backed by damp slacks, dunes and marsh, much of which is managed by Cheshire Wildlife Trust. Here is a wealth of wildflowers, butterflies, and the rare Natterjack Toad.

In the summer, Sea Holly, with its blue-purple spiked leaves, grows on the sandy dunes. Shown here, a Grayling butterfly feeds on the flowers.

Shown on old maps as both Red Stones and Red Rocks, this tip of the peninsula is a great place for big skies and wide horizons. On gentle summer evenings the fine sands stretch out to limitless places, a place for kite-flying, castle-building, or just for sitting dreaming. In wild winter storms, the incoming tide races across the wide sands towards the rocks, to crash and churn on promontories, ledges and crags.

Looking east towards Hoylake and the north Wirral coast from Red Rocks.

OPPOSITE
Wind turbines have, in recent years, become a familiar eyesore off the Wirral coast, with yet more of the monstrosities to come, thus ruining that special sense of place that was one of the great attractions of the landscape.

The Red Arrows often perform their aerobatic displays for crowds at the annual Hoylake Lifeboat Open Day in late August.

Red Rocks Marsh at high summer, the dunes and slacks adorned with wild flowers.

Clubhouse and course of the Royal Liverpool Golf Club. These fine links have hosted the Open Championship recently and are scheduled to do so again.

'The Hoylake of today is populous and flourishing. Save only on the sandhills, where they look across to Wales, rows of houses stretch along the edges of the links. The links itself, which has been the breeding-ground of champions, is generally recognised as the finest golf course in Britain. The Hoylake of 1869, the year in which golf came to rouse it from its pleasant drowsiness, was a very different place. Let us imagine ourselves sitting on the grass, where now is the clubhouse. Over against us there would have been the Royal Hotel, without the club rooms that were afterwards added. To the right of the Royal would have been two houses, Chase East and Chase West, which are still there, and farther to the right again one or two cottages. There would have been no other habitation to be seen, and at our backs fields would have stretched unbroken to West Kirby. Between us and the Royal there would have been the posts of the racecourse making a circuit around what is now the practising ground called The Field. Twice a year, on the occasion of the races, Hoylake presumably became a gay spot. Otherwise the rabbits must have had it largely to themselves.'

(John Brownbill, *West Kirby and Hilbre*, 1928)

'Shops with glass-covered colonnades, smooth asphalted roads where the blown sand lies in ridges – delightfully clean dirt – a long, ever-growing promenade, rows of neat lodging-houses and tree-lined streets are what we find in Hoylake today. How different all this is from the scattered, sand-buried village, smelling strongly of shrimps, where the cocklers once lived on the shore of Hyle Lake. Hoylake has grown, but its old industry is by no means dead, for women and men still rake for fluted cockles on the banks.'

(T. A. Coward, *Picturesque Cheshire*, 1903)

OPPOSITE TOP
Detail from the sculpture in Station Road.

OPPOSITE BELOW
Ornate Victorian drinking-fountain on the promenade.

BELOW
The entrance to Hoylake is adorned by this modern sculpture featuring the seabirds that are such a prominent feature of this seaside town.

OPPOSITE RIGHT
A remnant of old maritime Hoylake: the lighthouse in Valentia Road, behind the promenade.

Meols

'A kind of serenity is produced by a ridge of sands some miles in length. It rises in the ocean about half a mile from the shore, and is opposite to the downs. The sea, thus divided from the main, is properly enough termed Lake, but whereof the epithet High is added, it might, perhaps, be difficult to say. The spring-tides entirely cover this sandy eminence twice in the 24 hours, but their ebb leaves a part of it visible. The glassy smoothness of this marine lake affords charming bathing for cowards. Near the coast the sands are admirably firm and smooth, two or three miles in extent, right and left. Whether the waters of the Dee and of the Mersey flowing into this lake do or do not somewhat abate its saline properties, is disputed. They seem, to my taste, less salt than those of the north coast, but exhibit the varied tints of the ocean.'

(Anna Seward, 1794)

Moreton

This old lighthouse has been in the background of my life since childhood. From my home in Moreton I could see the top of the tower peeking up from the line of embankment. As a youngster I would cycle down lovely old Lingham Lane on summer days, its hedges filled with honeysuckle and wild roses, for a peek through the rusty keyhole into the dark recesses of its cobweb-lined interior. I would lie in the long, flower-filled grasses at its base and gaze up to its dizzy heights, dreaming of and imagining the days when this, one of the oldest lighthouse sites in England, offered a much-needed warning to mariners sailing out in the perilous waters of Liverpool Bay.

Back in the early 1980s, a sad period when it was locked and abandoned, neglected by all and in danger of ruination, I said of the lighthouse: 'The briny winds have turned its once-white exterior a dirty grey, and it now looks worse than ever. I expect little remains of the building's seven floors, or the cast-iron staircase winding up to the lighthouse space, 101 feet above ground – only dust and cobwebs.'

Shortly after I wrote those words, local folk decided to take action by forming the Friends of Leasowe Lighthouse, and the old tower now stands proud again, lovingly restored and regularly open to visitors.

Wallasey and New Brighton

'The village of Wallasey, which consists principally of one street, is situated on the summit of an elevated ridge that commands a beautiful view over Bidston and the Leasowes, a level tract several miles in extent, which commences immediately under the village and reaches the sea. The inroads of the waters on this coast have been so serious and so constant, as to create the greatest alarm for the safety of the low lands, which are below the level of the sea at the highest spring tides.

The Wallasey Leasowe was probably the oldest gentleman's race-course in the kingdom, being noticed as existing in the early part of the seventeenth century. The races at Rood-eye at Chester, or at Smithfield and other places, were comparatively the sports of a mere fair, and could offer no rivalry to the aristocratic amusements of the Leasowe course, which in 1683 had rather an illustrious jockey, in the person of the famous Duke of Monmouth.'

(William Mortimer, *A History of the Hundred of Wirral*, 1847)

Leasowe Castle sits beside the sea between the sand-dunes and the golf course on the windswept, low-lying plain that was home to the nationally famous 'Wallasey Races'. It was built in 1593 by Ferdinando, Fifth Earl of Derby, as a fortified house, and has been extended and altered very many times over the past 400 years. Today it is a hotel and conference centre, rescued in the nick of time in the 1980s from decay and dereliction.

'It is a curious place, this New Brighton, a lesser Blackpool, with its promenade, pier and lofty tower. The fort which stands beside the lighthouse on a red rock is far more picturesque than effective. As a watering-place New Brighton is hardly a success; Lancashire trippers do bathe here, but one must walk far to get knee-deep. There is, however, much healthy paddling going on, both young and old gloating in the cool, though somewhat Liverpool-stained water. Donkey- and horse-riding is a great source of amusement, especially to spectators, and then there is all the attraction of the pier. There is a promenade, too, other than the pier; "Ham and Egg Terrace" is its name. Coy maidens lure the pleasure-seeker to enter their gaudy saloons, where oysters, shrimps, aerated waters and other luxuries may be partaken of, but at one and all the stock dish is ham and eggs. Do not enquire where the eggs come from. There are other entertainments on the terrace; you can have your photograph taken and printed while you wait, then there are penny gaffs, menageries, peep-shows, performing dogs and boxing cats, ventriloquists and all the other charms of the tripper's seaside resort.'

(T. A. Coward, *Picturesque Cheshire*, 1903)

The first sights to greet visitors entering the Mersey by sea are the lighthouse and Fort Perch Rock Battery. The 'little Gibraltar of the Mersey' was built between 1826 and 1829 to protect Liverpool from invasion – the Napoleonic Wars having posed a serious theat to England's security. It is now a museum.

New Brighton lighthouse stands alongside the Fort, sharing the same outcrop of sandstone known in olden times as the 'Black Rock' – a hazard to Mersey shipping for centuries. Before the lighthouse was built, a 'perch' with a basket of flaming coals and rags warned mariners of the rock, but this was swept away by storms and high seas so often that something far more substantial was needed. The 90-foot-high lighthouse was built in 1827–30 of Anglesey granite, the stone blocks being dovetailed into each other and covered with pozzolano, a volcanic material from the slopes of Mount Etna, which sets rock-hard.

A few years ago the lighthouse was let out as accommodation for honeymoon couples, and a light of sorts has shone out across the estuary from here in recent times.

New Brighton's Marine Lake is undergoing change as new developments take place on its perimeter. As I write, scaffolding and cranes dominate the scene, and only time will tell if the 'new' New Brighton will revitalise this part of the Wirral Peninsula.

New Brighton owes its origins to Liverpool merchant James Atherton who, in the 1830s, bought 170 acres of what was then grassy, windswept, sandy heathland leading down to the wave-beaten shore, and built villas in spacious grounds, each with an uninterrupted view of the sea and estuary. His prospectus for the estate makes the properties seem very desirable: 'New Brighton is situated at the Rock Point, three miles distant from Liverpool, and from its elevated situation commands from all points the most interesting and extensive views. The Welsh Mountains, the Orme's Heads and the Isle of Man are all distinctly visible. As a Bathing Place it has peculiar advantages, not only from its being the nearest point to the open Sea, but it also possesses the most beautiful

Beach, the Sands are hard and clean, free from Mud, Gravel, or Quicksands, they are many miles in extent and cannot be equalled for the purpose of Exercise, whether in Carriages, on Foot, or on Horseback. New Brighton also possesses a more interesting Sea View than any other Watering Place can boast, being constantly enlivened by the passing of vessels to and from the rich and flourishing Port of Liverpool, in many instances approaching so near as to admit of persons on the shore conversing with those on board. Among its other advantages may be enumerated the salubrity of the Air, the certain supply of purest Spring Water, the aspect of all the Rooms fronting the sea, enjoying the refreshing breeze, and sheltered from the oppressive

heat of the afternoon's sun, while its proximity to Liverpool, together with the certainty and safety of Steam Navigation, must tend to render New Brighton a most agreeable and desirable place of resort to the Nobility and Gentry of all the neighbouring Counties.'

The prophecy came true. For over 100 years New Brighton prospered. Every summer brought crowded beaches, folk coming from the mill-towns of industrial Lancashire and the Midlands for a taste of the seaside. The ferries were crowded with trippers from Liverpool. Theatres played to full houses, entertaining the crowds with famous names from show business. The water was 'as clean as the Mediterranean'. There were oyster-stalls, minstrels on the beach, and bathing-machines. Right up to the late 1950s the people came, until tastes changed and the trippers and holidaymakers came no more. For 50 years the resort simmered away doing nothing in particular; but the past few years have seen the tide start to swing again. The new Floral Pavilion has been described as 'one of England's most stunning and iconic structures', and is the start of a multi-million-pound scheme to regenerate the resort. W. Mortimer wrote of the youthful resort in the 1840s: 'The building continues, and the young colony of New Brighton promises to be, at no distant day, one of the most fashionable watering-places in this part of the kingdom.' Is history repeating itself?

South of New Brighton is Vale Park, a popular place in summer with its bandstand and flower-beds.

The Town Hall at Seacombe, Wallasey: a reminder of the days when Wirral was made up of autonomous Boroughs, each with its own town hall and administration to look after the needs of its citizens. Some would say it all worked better then, the smaller local authorities being friendlier and more accessible to residents than the current structure.

Egremont, one of the several once-tiny townships that eventually grew and combined to form the County Borough of Wallasey. Here was a ferry-crossing of the Mersey to Liverpool. Near here, too, was old 'Mother Redcap's', a notorious tavern run by a bohemian lady who served local mariners, smugglers and fishermen, turning a blind eye to the illicit trade taking place under her nose. 'Mother Redcap's' was demolished in the 1970s, with, legend has it, a stash of gold buried beneath its stones.

St Hilary's Church – the Parish Church of Wallasey – is a prominent landmark, marking one of the highest points in this part of Wirral.

Part of the New Brighton skyline seen from the seaward side of the Marine Lake.

'The dwelling-houses of Wallasey are 408 in number; and of these, four are fully licensed: the Ship Inn, Boat Inn, Black Horse, and the Cheshire Cheese – a new inn, which replaces the ancient and pcituresque house, for which it was claimed (probably inaccurately) that King William III slept a night there on his way to or from Ireland, a room in it being always shewn as that in which he slept. There are also seven beerhouses in the township. The district is noted for its market gardens, which are very numerous and excellent, and the early Wallasey potatoes were in great demand before the introduction of even earlier ones from the Channel Islands and abroad. There is also a small brewery, and Wallasey Mill used to be a famous landmark on the crest of the hill, but has lately been removed to make way for a new villa. Lying on the side of a sloping hill, it commands fine views and fresh sea breezes, and is sure to become a very popular place of residence now that speedy transit is afforded. Standing on the Slopes, or Breck, it is easy to recognise at once the truth and appropriateness of its name, Walea, "the wooded island",

which doubtless once reared its head from the surrounding waters which covered Leasowe plain and joined the estuary of the Mersey by way of the great Wallasey Pool.

The township of Liscard has increased 8,000 per cent in population since the century opened; its dwelling-houses have changed from 43 farmhouses and cottages to more than 3,000 dwellings of every kind, from mansions and villas downwards; a very remarkable growth, eclipsed only by its neighbour Birkenhead, but still worthy of note, and an instance of a wonderful vigour and vitality of the age we live in.

The portion of Liscard lying along the Mersey is known by the name of Egremont, and was "founded" by Mr John Askew, in 1835, as a watering-place for Liverpool. Although it has failed to fulfil its mission, it has yet become a very favourite residence, with villas and houses of a good class along the shore. In the neighbourhood of the ferry, Egremont is busy and thriving, with good shops.'

(Philip Sulley, *The Hundred of Wirral*, 1889)

REFLECTIONS ALONG THE MERSEY BANK

'On the grey surface of the Mersey estuary, approached by deep-water channels, well-lighted and buoyed, craft of all types and descriptions present an ever-changing scene of shipping activity which is probably unsurpassed in the world. All day long the tide of traffic ebbs and flows – the huge overtowering ocean liners, the coastwise ships, the ferry-boats, the coalers, the barges, the lighters – all jostling each other in the tideway like throngs in a city street. Its vessels venture forth to the four corners of the globe, returning richly laden with the produce of every clime. And these ships of trade, as they pass to and fro on their peaceful errand, seem sometimes like shuttles in a vast loom weaving a web of international prosperity and goodwill, which we pray no subtlety of the devil or of man may destroy or tear asunder.'

MERSEY magazine, 1921

The Western Gateway, they used to call it. This great river which dominates Wirral's eastern edge was the life-blood to all who lived and worked here. Her influence extended far beyond her granite banks: this was a symbol of Empire, her waters taking and fetching wealth from the four corners of the globe. This wealth helped shape Wirral as we know it today, and these briny waters which wash Wirral's shores have been both a barrier and a life-giving artery to the peninsula. A barrier which has kept Wirral separate from the port upon which so many have been dependent for their livelihood; and an artery without which Wirral might have remained a backwater.

To me, the Mersey has always existed. I cannot recall a time when it has not been part of my awareness. As a child I played upon Seacombe's sandy beaches, conscious even then of the pulsating rhythms of the mighty waters breaking on the rocks below. My school-years were spent within sight, sound and smell of the River Mersey: dank, grey November mists drifted up from the river to permeate our equally grey playground and classrooms. The tuneless notes of music lessons were accompanied on such days by the similarly cheerless wails of foghorns sounding across the river. On January days of howling gales we would daringly dodge the mighty waves splashing high over the promenade wall down by old Mother Redcap's, to return after lunch-hour to our lessons, our school uniforms drenched with Mersey brine.

Later years brought the excitement of New Brighton – the attractions of fairground and tower, and of romantic strolls along the prom on dusky summer evenings, arm-in-arm with the girl of the moment. Even then the Mersey predominated: silver moonlight and the pin-point lights of Liverpool reflecting off the placid, lake-like waters, ruffled only by the occasional crossing of a ferry-boat. Far out towards the Bar, the channel lights flashed intermittently, the Bar light itself shining over all.

And the river is, to me, still a mighty thing. Whether sailing across its waters on the ferry-boats, passing idle hours on its grassy banks at Eastham, or briskly walking its promenades at Wallasey, the Mersey still rates highly in my reflections of Wirral.

I love the ferries. Not many left now, alas, compared with years ago. The old landing-places make a long list: New Brighton, Egremont, Poulton, Seacombe, Woodside, Monks', Birkenhead, Tranmere, Rock, New and Eastham. Some have ancient origins, and the hazards of the primitive river-crossing are well described by travellers such as Celia Fiennes who crossed the estuary in 1698 and stated that it was 'hazardous to strangers to sail in the winter . . . it is of great breadth and at low water is so deep and salt as the sea . . . the waves toss and the great rocks all round it as dangerous as the sea'. A far cry from the comfort and convenience of today's Mersey crossing, which is a delightful experience at all times and in all seasons.

It's from the ferry-boats that we get the best impressions of our Wirral bank: man-made all the way up to Eastham, where the trees overhang the rocky low cliffs. Difficult to visualise how it looked 200 years ago, when the coast about Wallasey was described as being 'sandy and barren, and the only trees that existed grew close to the mouth of the river near the shore. There was scarcely a house between the Rock and Wallasey'.

As I read those words I think of the changes now taking place along these Wirral shores: the regeneration of old docklands into marinas and leisure centres. In a brief span of only 200 years the Mersey edge of our peninsula has changed almost beyond recognition.

Yet still the river ebbs and flows twice a day; still its waters – cleaner than they have been for decades – wash Wirral's shores: today, gently, silently; tomorrow, hurtling and crashing before violent seas. The flow of these tides always continues. As now, so in prehistoric time long, long before these floating-stages, these docks and far-converging ships, long before these iron piers ran out from the Cheshire shore – before, and long, long after them was, and shall ever be, this restless Mersey.

Birkenhead

They used to bathe, ride donkeys, and gather periwinkles on Birkenhead beach in the olden days. That was a long time ago – when meadow-lands swept down from the heights of Claughton Common, Oxton and Tranmere to the banks of the Mersey. Then, the Birkenhead edge of the Mersey was a tumble of rocky headlands clothed in greenery: high tides lapped against ferns and wild-flowers, and birch-branches dipped leaves and twigs into briny waters. Hard to picture it today, though. The hotels, the beaches, the greenery – it's all gone. Swept away when Laird built his shipbuilding yards here 150 years ago. That, really, was the end of the birchen heads, and the beginning of Birkenhead.

Pioneering. That's the word that springs to mind when I think of Birkenhead. The great river which touches this town's edge sent many folk westwards across the Atlantic, to start new lives in new lands, thousands of miles away. But other pioneers came only half-a-mile across the turbulent Mersey waters, or from across the Irish Sea, to settle in Birkenhead and found this new place. They came with nothing but a vision of a better future for themselves and their families; and they carved roads, railways and buildings on these green Mersey banks . . . 'One of the facts which have most deeply impressed us lately is the sudden rise of a new city in England. We allude to Birkenhead on the Mersey . . . one of the greatest wonders of the age . . . the grandest monument which the nineteenth century has erected to the genius of Commerce and Peace.' Prophetic words indeed!

Birkenhead is a place of firsts – England's first public park, the first tramway service, the first public library. This town had everything going for it. It should have arisen to become one of Europe's most important, most beautiful cities. But it didn't. Perhaps it is too close to Liverpool – Birkenhead never got a chance to develop its own personality.

Wonderful waterfront – and getting better all the time. Have you seen sunrise over the Liverpool skyline on autumn mornings, with the little ferry-boats scuttling across the gold-crested waters to Liverpool? And majestic Hamilton Square: the formality of its buildings beautifully matched by the symmetry of its neat lawns and colourful flower-beds. A real study in Victorian splendour and foursquare Victorian values. In contrast, Birkenhead Park's great attraction is its very unpredictability. What a superb blend of woodland and water, grassland and gardens. And odd buildings – boathouse, bridge, lodges – glimpsed through the greenery of beech branches and rhododendron bushes.

This all seems far removed from those riverside places down by the old Priory, where it all started. Those ancient stones, so rudely awakened from their slumbers by the coming of commerce a century and a half ago – they've seen the fortunes of man rise and fade, as the wind on the Mersey and the very tide itself.

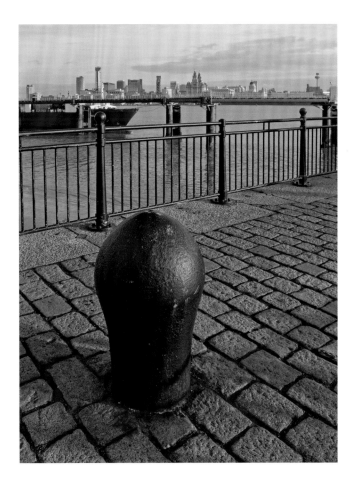

The Williamson Art Gallery and Museum has built a strong regional reputation for the quality and variety of its exhibitions and houses most of Birkenhead's art and history collections.

The art collection is the largest, numbering some 6,000 oil paintings, watercolours, drawings and prints; the collection's strengths lie in British works, especially by artists with local connections.

In addition there are important collections of local ceramics, especially Birkenhead's own Della Robbia Pottery (1894–1906) and eighteenth-century Liverpool porcelain.

Hamilton Square and Birkenhead Town Hall, built in the 1850s and described by a writer at the time as 'a beautiful quadrangle of about seven acres, scarcely excelled by any buildings in the kingdom. It is surrounded on every side by elegant stone-fronted houses, four storeys high, in the doric style of architecture, rusticated as far as the first-storey course, the wing house having four bold columns in front, supporting a handsome frieze and parapet. The gardens are enclosed by iron railings and are tastefully laid out for the special use of the occupants.'

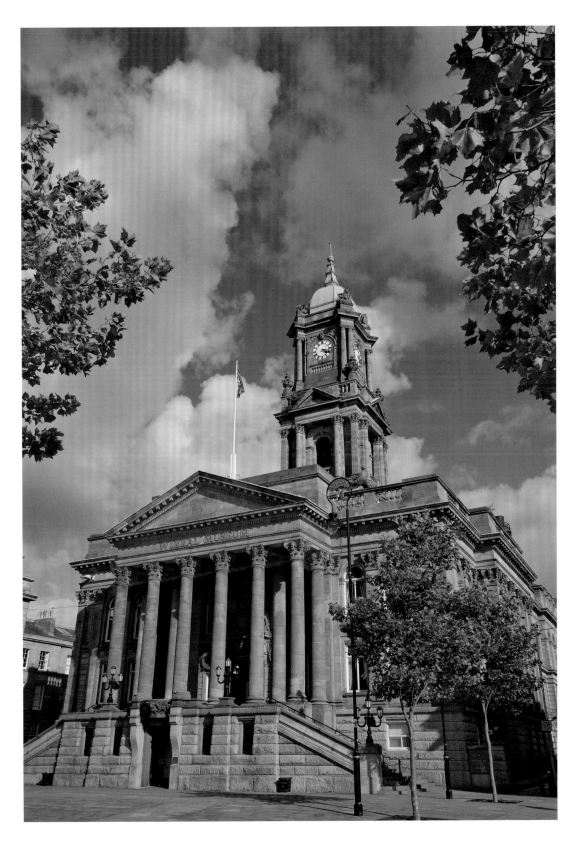

Birkenhead Town Hall, on the south side of Hamilton Square. The opening ceremony was performed in February 1887 by John Laird, the Borough's first Mayor. It is built of Storeton stone and Scottish granite and marble. With local government reorganisation in the 1970s, the building was no longer needed as a town hall, and eventually became the Wirral Museum. However, in 2009 it was advertised by the Council for sale or lease to someone with 'the vision and expertise to shape the future of a landmark building at the heart of one of England's finest public squares'. It asked for 'expressions of interest from individuals and organisations who can show they can provide a sustainable use for the former Birkenhead Town Hall'. The advert said that the building 'provides a fitting focal point for one of England's grandest public squares – only Trafalgar Square in London can boast more Grade 1 listed buildings than Hamilton Square. Its stunning interior includes magnificent civic rooms, beautiful stained glass, colourful hand-crafted tiles and a sweeping grand staircase with pink marble balustrades. The building can rival the finest Victorian civic decoration.' At the time of writing, its future is still undecided.

The Boathouse, Birkenhead Park. The park was conceived as part of the overall plan for the development of Birkenhead town in the 1830s, but was designed by Sir Joseph Paxton, the celebrated landscape gardener, to offer a complete contrast to the structured rectangular grid layout of the town. Paxton turned 'a low, foul-smelling swamp' into a park which would contain 'extensive drives, beautiful walks and elegant gardens, adorned with groves, fountains, ornamental waters and numerous sources of pleasure'. The park was opened in 1847 by Sir William Jackson amid scenes of great rejoicing and celebration; the day was declared a public holiday, and the whole town made the most of the occasion. Paxton's design for the park was used as a basis for other public parks in England, and Olmsted borrowed some of Paxton's ideas for the creation of Central Park, New York.

OVERLEAF
The Swiss Bridge, Birkenhead Park.

OVERLEAF, RIGHT
Detail from the Boathouse, Birkenhead Park.

A corner of Oxton village, one of Birkenhead's many leafy suburbs.

Gentlemen enjoying a game of bowls at Oxton Conservative Club.

The Cheshire historian George Ormerod described Oxton in the early 1800s: 'The village of Oxton is mean and small, composed of wretched straggling huts, amongst roads impassable. The township occupies an eminence which commands a full view of the buildings and shipping of Liverpool, exhibiting a picture resembling metropolitan bustle and splendour, almost immediately below the eye; but no degree of civilisation or improvement has reached this part of the opposite shore, which is a scene of solitude, broken in upon only by the voice of the cowherd or the cry of the plover. Bleak and barren moors stretch round it in every direction and exhibit an unmixed scene of poverty and desolation.' All was to change, though, for by the turn of the century Coward was writing: 'Fine streets lead up the hill from Birkenhead to Oxton, and the higher we rise, the more we leave the town behind and the more residential the district becomes, till on the eminence, where there is a splendid view of Birkenhead, the river and Liverpool, we have a most desirable suburb of good houses built in a fine, healthy neighbourhood.'

Many gardens in Oxton are open to the public in May each year under the 'Oxton Secret Gardens' scheme, giving owners and gardeners a chance to show off their plots to visitors, while at the same time raising money for local charities.

Port Sunlight

'My father was 36 years of age when he decided to seek a fresh site with more ideal conditions for the further development of his (soap) business. Coming over to Birkenhead, they made their way through Rock Ferry to New Ferry, and, walking in a southerly direction, were soon in country lanes and open fields. The picturesque village of Lower Bebington – now so rapidly becoming suburban – was then an almost isolated country hamlet. The main railway line from Birkenhead to Chester passes just to the east of Bebington, and the country between this railway line and the River Mersey where the village of Port Sunlight now stands was in those days composed of open fields and marshes, with some blocks of squalid and ill-kept cottage property bordering on New Ferry. Lever and his architect were walking with their backs to Birkenhead across the fields I have referred to, when they came to a gate – the spot was a few yards in front of where now stands the main entrance to Lever Brothers' offices – and there they saw before them the very land they had been looking for. To their right ran the main railway line from Birkenhead to London, and a few hundred yards to their left a muddy tidal creek wound its way to the Mersey. "Here we are," said Lever, "this is the site I will choose."

The ceremony of cutting the first sod was performed by Mrs Lever on 3 March 1888. The invited guests assembled on the Liverpool landing-stage and crossed to New Ferry by steamer, from where they were taken in a steam barge up the tidal creek to the site of the new works, which Lever had decided to name "Port Sunlight". In the evening a banquet was held at the Bear's Paw restaurant in Liverpool, and in the course of his speech at the dinner, Lever said: "It is my hope and my brother's hope, some day, to build houses in which our work-people will be able to live and be comfortable – semi-detached houses, with gardens back and front, in which they will be able to know more about the science of life than they can in a back slum, and in which they will learn that there is more enjoyment in life than in the mere going to and returning from work and looking forward to Saturday night to draw their wages".

(The Second Viscount Leverhulme, 1927)

The Lady Lever Art Gallery, built by William Hesketh Lever during 1914–22 as a memorial to his wife, Elizabeth Ellen.

The War Memorial, Port Sunlight. Designed by William Goscombe John, it takes the form of a runic cross in granite, with a group of bronze figures at its foot – soldiers defending women and children. Around the base is a parapet with bas-relief groups representing the Services. The four approaches to the parapet are flanked by eight sculptured groups of children. At the unveiling ceremony, Leverhulme said of the designer: 'He has produced sermons in stone and metal that will teach us our duty without humiliating or lecturing us'. The architectural writer Edward Hubbard said: 'it provides a fair example of a war memorial which is genuinely moving and which avoids sentimentality'.

OPPOSITE
The Lyceum and Dell bridge. This corner of Port Sunlight was described in the 1950s: 'A gracious dell, once the bed of a forgotten rivulet, winds through one corner of the estate . . . throughout, levels change in a pleasing way. Some of this is God-given, some of it the work of architects who had the humility to add to existing enchantments instead of seeking to trick and tease with mere virtuosity.'

OVERLEAF
Typical corners of Port Sunlight village, showing the variety yet harmonious nature of the styles of domestic architecture.

Bebington

'Bebington – the very name visualises a quaintly winding street of irregular roofs, leading up to broad tree-shaded roads, and rising clear above the branches is the soaring spire of the old church.' That was way back at the turn of the nineteenth century. The soaring spire is still there but the quaintness, sadly, has gone. Bebington is now a pleasant place in which to live, with few reminders of the past. It's sandwiched between the Mersey and the mid-Wirral countryside, with part of it low-lying, and part extending up towards the Storeton ridge.

What is nice, though, are the occasional glimpses of the River Mersey seen between the houses. Nathaniel Hawthorne, who stayed here as American Ambassador to Liverpool 150 years ago, was not so endeared to the river, which he thought would be 'a pleasanter object, if it were blue and transparent, instead of such a mud-puddly hue'.

Yet there are occasions when, under blue skies and placid conditions, this broad, almost lake-like part of the river does indeed seem blue and transparent. Walk along the old esplanade on such a day, and see what I mean.

St Andrew's Parish Church sits quietly in a leafy backwater of the village – 'one of the finest old churches in Wirral', with Saxon foundations. But if you are worried about problems such as the end-times of the world and doomsday, then take a quick peek at the ivy climbing the church-tower. A legendary prophecy suggests that when the ivy at Bebington church reaches the top of the spire, then the end of the world will be nigh. We've little to worry about for a good few years yet – on my last visit I could find only a small piece twineing around the base of the tower!

The porch,
St Andrew's
Parish Church.

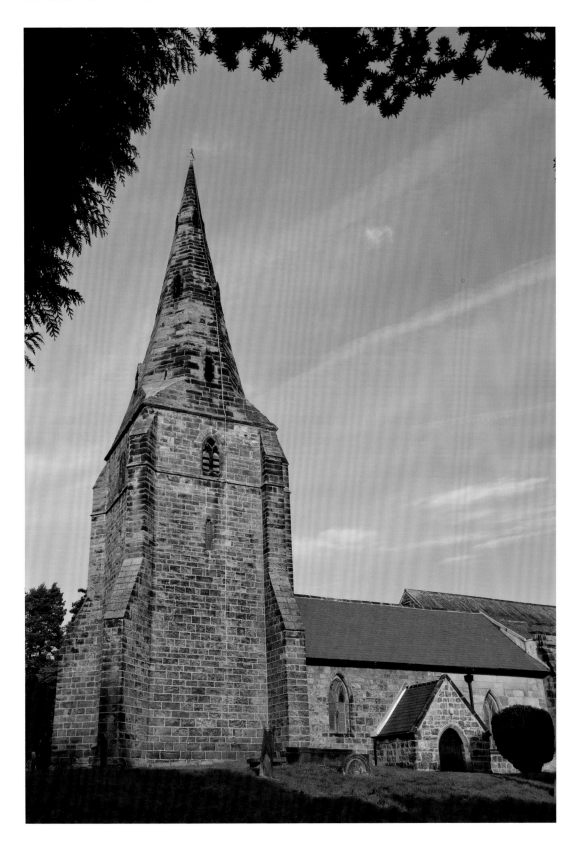

St Andrew's Church, Bebington. In August 1853, while living locally as American Consul in Liverpool, the American Nathaniel Hawthorne took a walk to Bebington and its church: 'Yesterday we all took a walk into the country. The ramble was very pleasant along the hedge-lined roads, in which there were flowers blooming. The bell of the old church was ringing as we went along, and many respectable-looking people and cleanly dressed children were moving towards the sound. Soon we reached the church, and I have seen nothing yet in England that so completely answered my idea of what such a thing was, as this old village church of Bebbington. It is quite a large edifice, built in the form of a cross, a low peaked porch in the side, over which, rudely cut in stone, is the date 1300 and something. The steeple has ivy on it, and looks old, old, old; so does the whole church, though portions of it have been renewed, but not so as to impair the aspect of heavy, substantial endurance, and long, long decay, which may go on hundreds of years longer before the church is a ruin. There it stands, among the surrounding graves, looking just the same as it did in Bloody Mary's days; just as it did in Cromwell's time.'

Eastham

'Eastham is the finest old English village I have seen, with many antique houses, and with altogether a rural and picturesque aspect . . . there were thatched stone cottages mixed with houses of a better kind . . . it was not merely one long wide street, but there were several crooked ways, gathering the whole settlement into a pretty small compass.'

Nathaniel Hawthorne wrote those words 150 years ago. At the time he was American Consul to Liverpool but living in Wirral, and this is but one of many word-portraits he painted of these villages dotted about the Mersey bank.

Folk pass through Eastham on their way to the old Ferry and Country Park. A few of them stop off to search out the fascinating history behind the buildings we see today. Even fewer track down the oldest living thing in Wirral; they find it in the corner of the churchyard – a venerable yew tree. How old is it? everyone asks. Perhaps 1,500 years old, says the plaque affixed to the tree. How it survives, with its gaping hollow trunk, I really don't know!

There's quite a lot else to see in Eastham besides the yew tree; take a look at the church, for a start, with its rare broached spire; then look at the old cottages and inns – and imagine Eastham as it was in the days when two dozen or more stage-coaches a day passed through en route to the Ferry, bringing passengers to the Liverpool boats from Chester and beyond.

Eastham is close enough to the River Mersey to occasionally have the salt-tang of the sea in the air, when the breeze blows up from the east. On such occasions it is easier to visualise the days when Eastham's fortunes were more closely tied to the river – when her folk eked out livings from the tide's flooding and ebbing, either as fisher-folk landing their catch, or as boatmen and innkeepers whose livelihood depended on the wayfarers who passed through the village.

They, of course, have long since gone; but the river remains, passing by this ancient village as if it did not exist.

TOP
Detail from the old ticket office, Eastham Ferry.

BELOW
Eastham Ferry: the old ticket office and the Ferry Hotel. There was a ferry across the Mersey from Eastham, known then as Job's Ferry, as early as the sixteenth century. In the middle years of the nineteenth century the ferry area was developed as 'a place of resort' for day-trippers from Lancashire. The 'Richmond of the Mersey', as it became known, boasted zoological gardens showing bears, monkeys, lions and tigers; the old bear-pit, monkey cages and fountains can still be traced among the rhododendrons. The area is now Eastham Country Park, a popular place for picnics and strolls through the woods.

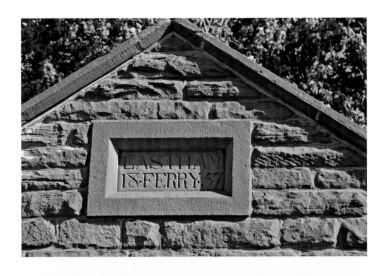

Eastham Woods is a delightful place in which to stroll at any time of the year, especially in spring when bluebells carpet the floor.

Ellesmere Port

The town grew from nothing (a census of 1801 shows only 25 families living here) to become the largest industrial town in Cheshire in less than 200 years. Its beginnings were the result of the construction of the Ellesmere Canal – part of a network of canals linking the Severn, the Mersey and the Dee. Such a scheme, it was said, would 'enable the wares of Shropshire to reach the sea, and at the same time provide better transport for the coal and iron

of the Wrexham area and the minerals and agriculture of the Welsh borders.'

The National Waterways Museum was created in the 1970s at a time when the canal docks and associated warehousing and other buildings were rapidly decaying. It is now one of England's best museums, and always worth a visit.

Cameos from the National Waterways Museum ('The Boat Museum'), Ellesmere Port.

MID-WIRRAL REFLECTIONS

'If ever the reader finds himself at Hooton, and the day appears to promise well, let him turn along the road which runs west to the ancient little village of Willaston, and go soon, for the building spirit is in the air, and land has acquired a building-land value, so that men who bought it by the acre will now offer it to you by the yard. The district is such an agreeable one to dwell in that it is certain to lose, in the not-distant future, the pleasant flavour of an out-of-the way place.'

HAROLD YOUNG, 1909

Willaston village.

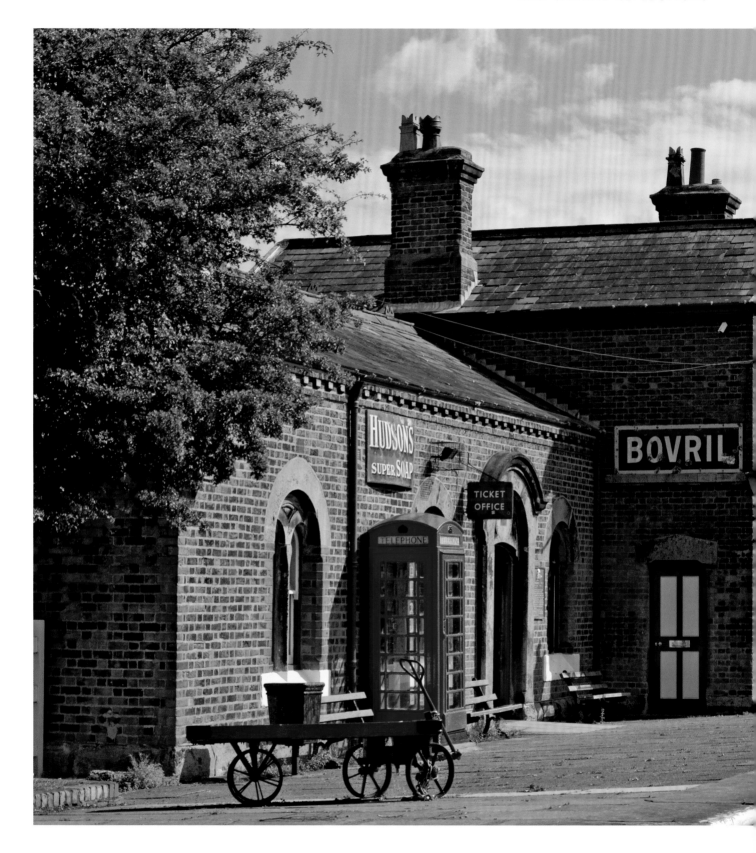

The old railway station, Hadlow Road, on the western outskirts of Willaston. This is the only station in Wirral Country Park to have retained its original platform buildings. 'Step inside the Waiting Room and you are transported back to a bygone age. Everything is just as it was on a typical working day in 1952. Ticket racks, date stamps, oil lamps and the associated paraphernalia which only railway offices can accumulate – all are here, not neatly laid out for display but cosily untidy. Even a fire burns in the grate. All that is missing is the sound of the train approaching the platform . . .'

BELOW
The plaque on the station building conjures up the atmosphere of a typical working day 60 years ago.

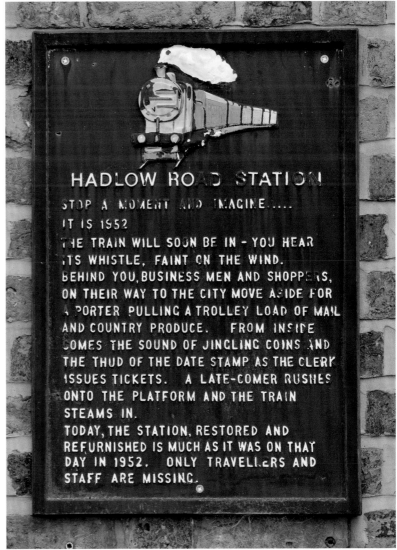

HADLOW ROAD STATION
STOP A MOMENT AND IMAGINE.....
IT IS 1952
THE TRAIN WILL SOON BE IN - YOU HEAR
ITS WHISTLE, FAINT ON THE WIND.
BEHIND YOU, BUSINESS MEN AND SHOPPERS,
ON THEIR WAY TO THE CITY MOVE ASIDE FOR
A PORTER PULLING A TROLLEY LOAD OF MAIL
AND COUNTRY PRODUCE.   FROM INSIDE
COMES THE SOUND OF JINGLING COINS AND
THE THUD OF THE DATE STAMP AS THE CLERK
ISSUES TICKETS.   A LATE-COMER RUSHES
ONTO THE PLATFORM AND THE TRAIN
STEAMS IN.
TODAY, THE STATION, RESTORED AND
REFURNISHED IS MUCH AS IT WAS ON THAT
DAY IN 1952.   ONLY TRAVELLERS AND
STAFF ARE MISSING.

Bromborough and Raby Mere

The people of Bromborough are among the luckiest in Wirral, for they have on their doorstep this tangled wilderness of wooded river valleys, wet meadows and Wirral's largest sheet of water. These river valleys radiate from Raby Mere like spokes from a wheel – ancient, native woodlands rich in flowers that have taken centuries to root and spread. Can there be a sight more glorious than these bluebell woods in spring – a shimmering haze of blue filling the air with that pervasive perfume so characteristic of these wild hyacinths?

But not only the woods, the brooks and the meadows – Raby Mere too. Hard to believe that this is not a natural lake – so well does it blend in with the surrounding woods and pastures. Long ago the brook was dammed up for the water mill below, and thus Raby Mere was formed. The works of man are rarely as beautiful as this, and the place was aptly described by a rambler a hundred years ago: 'Nowhere else is there such a varnish on the holly hedges, and bluebells crowd so thickly around your feet that you shrink from treading down the azure belfry. Tea can be obtained at every cottage in the dale; but not on Sunday – neither crumb nor crust nor cup can you get for fear, love or money. Raby Mere still remains the same sylvan glade, so closely interwoven with the golden memories of youth and childhood.'

The Wheatsheaf Inn, Raby village – a popular hostelry for Wirral folk. Raby is probably the limit or boundary of the early Norse settlers in Wirral who gave Scandinavian names to so many Wirral settlements. A rambler 100 years ago described the old place thus: 'Raby Village, its walls as grey-green as the trunks of its apple-trees, is quietly prosperous. Its centre is the Wheatsheaf Inn, a thick-walled old house standing away from the road on a stoney causeway. The sight of this old place, with its quaint sign, low-browed ingle and cavernous stone stairways, is sufficient to stir a very somnolent imagination. It has stood facing the moorland wind for years, and there is no reason why it should not so stand for centuries to come unless (and such crimes are not unknown) it should be deliberately razed to the ground.'

The Wirral countryside is dotted with these attractive footpath direction signs, most of which were erected by the Wirral Footpaths and Open Spaces Preservation Society, a voluntary organisation dedicated to looking after the many hundreds of miles of public footpaths which criss-cross the peninsula. This is in Brimstage village and points the rambler in the direction of Thornton Hough.

Thornton Hough

The rural heart of Wirral boasts a number of nucleated villages bounded by fields, copses and woodland: Storeton, Raby, Brimstage and others. None, though, fits the picture of the typical English village so much as Thornton Hough, with its large village green bounded by picturesque black-and-white half-timbered houses and cottages, churches and village blacksmith.

Most of the old village has long gone, its 'inferior' buildings swept away 125 years ago when, first, Joseph Hirst, a retired Yorkshire woollen merchant, and then the First Viscount Leverhulme recreated the village in their own styles of building. A rambling-man visiting Thornton Hough shortly after the village's reconstruction said, 'In their place has arisen one of the most charming villages of the English country scene.'

Winner of the 'Best Kept Village' award on a number of occasions, Thornton Hough has also been popular for its summer Scarecrow Festival, with home-made scarecrows adorning gardens of many homes in the village.

The village green, smithy, cottages, church and trees: the quintessentially English village – and planned as such by W. H. Lever a hundred years ago.

Purest Norman architecture down to the last detail; but Thornton Hough's St George's Church is not a thousand years old, but a hundred! The First Viscount Leverhulme commissioned the church, and insisted that no expense be spared in its attention to architectural detail – 'even to a stone altar with five consecrational crosses cut into its surface. The organ case was carved from oak taken from the house in Bolton in which Mrs Lever was born.'

With its graceful spire peeking through the trees, and using warm-red local sandstone, All Saints' is a prominent landmark seen from the surrounding countryside. This was built at the expense of Joseph Hirst in 1867 and is set on a fine site in the village, looking westwards over the expanse of the village green.

Note the two clocks on the eastern wall of the tower: apparently after the church was finished the vicar realised that he could not see the main clock from his vicarage and asked for a second face to be added above the main one so that he could get to his services on time!

Just outside the village, behind an imposing black-and-white half-timbered gatehouse, sits Thornton Manor, formerly home of the Leverhulmes but now a hotel and conference centre.

Right
On the other side of the village is Thornton Hall, a Victorian mansion that is now a popular hotel and sports club.

St George's Church,
Thornton Hough.

Brimstage

'A large portion of this township is situated in a plain, which by continued labour has been worked into a high state of cultivation. The long and very straggling village stands in a rather peculiar situation, the houses of which it is composed being placed on one side of a ravine which extends through the hamlet, and down the centre of which a rivulet runs.

Brimstage was the ancient settlement of the Domvilles, a house of high consideration among the gentry of Cheshire, most probably a junior branch of the Barons of Montalt. Brimstage Hall, long the residence of the Domvilles, and most probably of the later generations of the Troutbecks, is a stone edifice with many claims to attention. It stands on one side of the village, on a flat mound, of some elevation above the opposite buildings. It was formerly surrounded with a moat, varying from 14 to 20 yards in width. The hall, standing considerably above the rivulet, which is crossed by several small and very rude bridges, presents a pleasing subject for the pencil. In the original state of the fabric, it must have been of great strength and importance, and it presents one of the most perfect and ancient specimens of domestic architecture in this part of the county.

Attached to it is a very ancient square tower, of considerable height, and probably the ancient stronghold of the Hulses, of which this tower was the donjon or keep.'

(William Mortimer, *The History of the Hundred of Wirral*, 1847)

Arrowe Park and Woodchurch

'A level, green country spreads out before you . . . here and there along the dark ridge, trees are set like lace against a marigold sky . . . the wide pastures rich in the varying greens of the meadows and woods make a swift appeal to town-tired eyes . . . this Wirral vista is never more beautiful than in its cool green raiment of early June.' That was how Woodchurch and Arrowe appeared to a traveller coming down Prenton hill from Birkenhead almost a hundred years ago. Much has changed since then, with this part of Wirral now a huge residential district. Meadows and woods, though, are retained within the grounds of vast Arrowe Park, laid out by John R. Shaw almost 200 years ago. Here, gravelled paths meander through avenues of fine trees to rhododendron-bordered lake and splashing waterfall. And, 'from the rounded crest of the green hill you have now reached, there lies before you a beautiful varied view stretching out for many miles till land and sea seem to fade into the misty fold of the horizon'. The remnants of the ancient village of Woodchurch, with its early church, are a short walk from the main entrance-gates of Arrowe Park.

The Parish Church of Holy Cross, Woodchurch. The oldest part is the twelfth-century tower, while parts of the south aisle are fourteenth century. A hundred years ago Charles Budden described it thus: 'The fine old churches of Wirral certainly form one of its chief sources of interest, and of these Woodchurch, of ancient foundation, takes a prominent place in the affections of most people. It is a real, old-world building, a suitable background for such scenes as are depicted in the writings of Jane Austen or Washington Irving; a church redolent with the atmosphere of bygone times and with the sweet memories of the England that is perhaps now changing its placid character.'

Arrowe Hall, built for John R. Shaw in 1835 and greatly extended in the following decades. In 1876 'a very handsome billiard room and conservatory, and in 1880 a spacious entrance hall were added, and these serve for the display of an almost unique collection of stuffed animals and heads from all parts of the globe . . . among them are nine tigers, including a famous man-eater which had killed 600 cattle and men, women and children, and was pursued for nine days and nights before he fell to Captain Otho's unerring rifle.' (Sulley, *The Hundred of Wirral*, 1889)

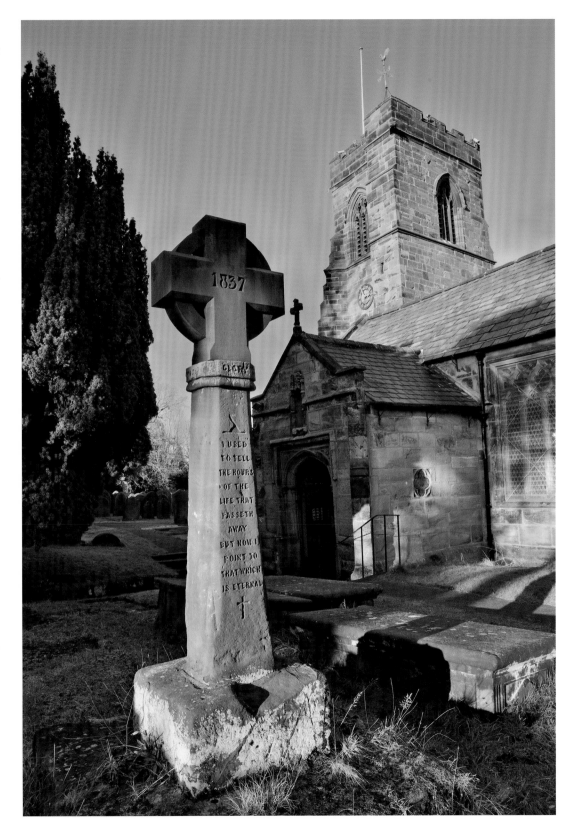

Great-spotted
Woodpecker, Arrowe
Park.

The Arrowe Brook,
Arrowe Park.

Bidston

'It was a little, quiet, grey village – so very grey indeed, and venerable, and quaint, that no flaunting red brick had dared to show itself and break the uniform tint of its gabled antiquity.' The adjectives which Albert Smith used 150 years ago to describe Bidston still apply – little, quiet, venerable, quaint. But its greyness overpowers – it's to do with the stone, of course, from which everything in the village is constructed – walls, cottages, old hall, church, all quarried from the local sandstone from the long ridge which begins here at Bidston and ends down Bebington way.

I suppose every local person over the age of 60 holds a sentimental image of the Bidston they knew before it was swallowed up by the march of time. With the adventure-land of the hill rearing up behind, it was the mecca for summer days out for families from the towns of Wallasey and Birkenhead. The scent of the countryside pervaded the air from the moment the steam-train pulled in at the station – the reed-beds of Bidston Moss extending away towards Wallasey hill; the squat, grey tower of Bidston church nestling among the trees; and may-blossom lanes leading enticingly up towards picnic-meadows and bluebell woods.

The hill is still a fascinating place. And the village? Well, the cottages, hall and church still survive as they ever did, and are probably in better condition now than for many years. You can still stare at the old Ring O'Bells Inn and imagine its oversized host, Simon the Cellarer, preparing his famed ham and eggs for the crowds at

holiday weekends ('on such occasions the inn yard would be crowded with gigs, spring-carts and traps of every description'). Or wonder at the architectural fascination of Church Farm, with its thirteen different floor levels. You can consider the aloofness of Bidston Old Hall, reposing high on its sandstone shelf above the village and once the home of the Stanleys who played such an important part in the Civil War.

OPPOSITE
Bidston Observatory.

BELOW
Panorama looking east from the ridge of Bidston Hill towards Liverpool.

PAGE 96
Bidston windmill.

PAGE 97 (TOP)
Parish church of St Oswald, Bidston.

PAGE 97 (BOTTOM)
The Lilacs, Bidston village.

Frankby and Royden Park

Frankby village is, to most folk, a 'passing-through' place, red-sandstone farm buildings beside the twisting road between Greasby and West Kirby. There's little reason to stop, for there are no shops – even the village store is no more. It has a village green, though, a pub, a huge cemetery, and is the gateway to Royden Park. This is no park in the usual sense, though – more a country park, for it's a place of woods and meadows and walks. Go on a Sunday, and as you arrive you'll hear the 'toot-toot' of steam engines scurrying back and forth through the woods and meadows, carrying mums and dads and youngsters on a five-minute ride on the miniature railway.

Hill Bark, on the edge of Royden Park and Thurstaston Hill. It was originally built on high ground near Bidston Hill, and transported and re-erected stone by stone on its present site in 1929. It was built in 1891 by Edward Ould, who said of it on completion: 'No style of building will harmonise so quickly and completely with its surroundings . . . and none continue to live on such terms of good fellowship with other materials, whether rosy brickwork, grey lichen-covered masonry, or pearly flag-slates, which last it loves the most of all. And then it is hard to say which season of the year most becomes it: in its cap of virgin snow, in its gorgeous garb of Virginia creeper, or in its purple veil of wisteria it is equally bewitching. At noonday it throws the broadest shadows, and at eve (as no other building can) it gathers on its snowy breast the rose of sunset, and responds to the silver magic of the moon.'

The walled garden, Royden Park. A place for all seasons: the laburnum arch in late spring, the wildflower meadows of summer, the tints of the falling leaves in autumn, and the frosty starkness of winter.

OVERLEAF
Sunrise over the Frankby woods and meadows.

DEESIDE REFLECTIONS

'The tide is out. Across the waste of wet sand comes the mournful wail of the curlew, almost the only sign of life. Away in the far distance a twinkling line of foam is crawling onwards; the fisherfolk at Gayton are manning their boats; the carts which have taken down the heavy nets are returning to the shore. The beacon buoy in the Deep swings round; Bug Swash swells till Big Ben is covered; and the far-off Caldy Blacks sink beneath the wave. The tide is coming. Parkgate Deep is full, and the boats at Heswall and Gayton strain on their anchors; guts are now broad rivers and bank after bank is lost beneath the racing waters, for the sea comes in apace across the flats.'

T. A. COWARD, 1903

The River Dee and its bordering pastures from the Thurstaston ridge.

Caldy

'The village consists of a collection of straggling fishermen's huts scattered over an eminence near the estuary, which is separated by a deep rocky valley from the parish of Thurstaston.'
(George Ormerod, *History of Cheshire*, 1819)

'The ascending road from West Kirby leads to Calday, now one of the prettiest hamlets in the county. On the hill, above the village, stood the beacon which formerly communicated with Everton, and with one on the opposite shore of the Dee; and between the Manor House and the school was the last existing maypole. There are some very picturesque old black-and-white houses, and everything in the small compass of this village seems quaintly beautiful.'
(Hilda Gamlin, *Twixt Mersey and Dee*, 1897)

'Caldy Hill is wild, untamed and wholly delightful. The keen eye will always find something of interest. The artist will enthuse over the play of cloud shadows across the banks and channels of the Dee, or, nearer to hand, the pure massed colours of golden gorse, mauve heath and purple heather. So many details will catch your eye: a lizard basking on a sun-warmed rock; the delicate tracery of self-sown silver birches; the antics of a red squirrel; the barbaric beauty of willow-herb in full flower; and, as summer merges into autumn, the indescribable tints of glowing bracken.'
(*West Kirby Guide*, 1951)

BELOW
Caldy from the air.
Caldy village nestles in
the trees at the centre,
with more recent
development below,
alongside the Wirral
Way. Caldy Golf Club
lies on either side of
the Wirral Way and
continues to the clay
cliffs beside the beach.
In the distance are the

flat, low-lying lands of
Newton, beyond which
lie the north Wirral
coastal communities of
Hoylake, Meols and
Moreton.

OPPOSITE
A fine day for a game
of cricket at the Caldy
Club below Thurstaston
Hill. Beyond is Caldy
Hill.

Caldy beach: a flock of
Godwit flies northwards
down the estuary as the
tide rises. Beyond, the
Welsh hills.

Thurstaston and Irby

'Thurstaston was always uplifted. From the beginning of time it sent all footpaths up to the ridge, and barely tolerated the Dee winding among the sandbanks below. The wise man leaves macadam far away, and by field-path and woodland, by farmyard and stile, by the grass-grown byway and the glade among tall trees, he drifts across Wirral to this last playground of paths' (W. T. Palmer, *The Verge of Wales*, 1942).

Palmer knew his Wirral well, and Thurstaston even better. He knew the magic of this heathland uplifted above the meadowlands bordering the silver Dee. He called it 'the place where the footpaths end', as rambling folk yesterday and today, from near and far, make for this land of big skies and wide-reaching views.

And he knew of Thor! 'He cribbed the toughest ridge in Wirral for foothold and played pitch-and-toss with boulders. From this 300-feet moor he looked out to sea past Hoylake, or up the river to Chester, as he desired. He was a standing figure, with health, strength and a jovial happiness which he has left as a legacy to all who venture on his open moor.'

Today, the stone of Thor's name is the Sunday-afternoon mecca of families, with children scrambling its foot-worn sides to the water-worn summit – new generations feeling the old, old magic of this place carved out of the crags, pools, woods and heaths of this uplifted land, 'the place where all footpaths end'.

ABOVE
The Parish Church of Thurstaston, St Bartholomew's, in its fine setting above the River Dee and distant prospect of Welsh hills.

BELOW
In the churchyard is the family grave of the Ismay family, owners of the White Star Line of *Titanic* fame. Thomas Henry Ismay lived in Thurstaston village from 1882 until his death in 1899 and inhabited a large mansion called 'Dawpool'; he helped fund a new school, but was also responsible for diverting the main highway through the new cutting, for closing the village inn, and for diverting the railway line away from the village towards the coast.

OPPOSITE
The tower of the previous church still stands in the churchyard of the present church. Behind the tower can be seen ancient Thurstaston Hall, parts of which go back a thousand years.

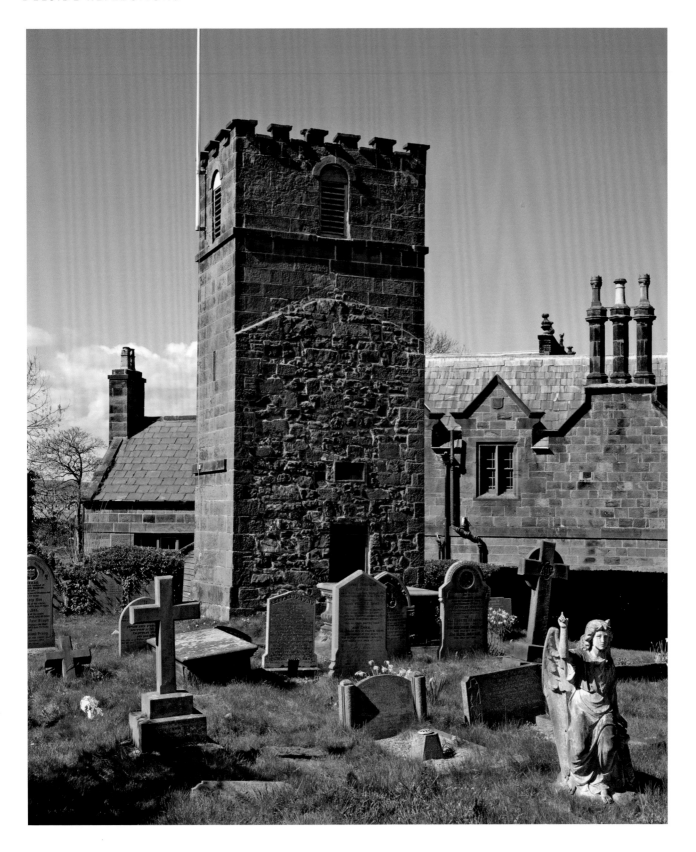

It is often said that the folk who founded our villages were looking for a warm, sheltered spot, well protected from their enemies, and with food and water supplies close by. Whoever chose Thurstaston all those centuries ago certainly found those things, but with an added bonus – a glorious view of the Dee and a panorama of the Welsh hills beyond.

The village stands proudly uplifted, nestling between the meadow-lands of Deeside and the craggy heaths of Thurstaston Common. The salt-winds sweep up from the estuary carrying the cries of gulls and oyster-catchers, to mingle here with the scent of gorse and heather off the heathland. And, always, there is the silver thread of the distant Dee seen through the trees, through the bare branches of winter, the fiery reds of autumn, and the gossamer green of spring.

A traveller in the early years of the last century described the approach to Thurstaston as he descended down from the Chester high road: 'From above the village a steep hill overarched with trees, between whose boughs we catch a lovely glimpse of the estuary of the Dee and the Welsh Hills, leads down to the flat lands below; at its foot on the left the church, the old hall and village; on the right, a thatched cottage standing in a garden gay with flowers, and the modern Dawpool Home Farm. Behind the cottage, a rocky bank covered with gorse, heather and broom blazes in summer; and between it and the church and hall, is spread a large green among the trees.'

Happily, Thurstaston has not suffered as one writer suggested 100 years ago. He commented on the beauty of the place, and wrote: 'A locality so favoured in America would have in no time sites marked out for public buildings, streets crowded with dwellings, with newspaper offices, churches, banks, a theatre or two, schools and other desirable institutions.'

Thurstaston Common is a lowland heath of woodland, heather- and gorse-clad heathland and damp, peaty hollows. Managed by the National Trust, it was saved from the builders' claws by Birkenhead Town Council way back in 1879 'having regard to the health, comfort and convenience of the inhabitants of Birkenhead and the benefit of the neighbourhood'. You will still find some of the old boundary-stones defining the Common's area.

A rambler 100 years ago described the heath: 'As you ascend, the sea wind mingling with the odours of pine and gorse intensifies the pleasure of the ramble, and reaching

the plateau, the landscape is more than merely interesting – a lonely moorland house, set amidst brown boulders, is suggestive of the rugged wilds of Devon or Ayrshire. From here the land slopes into broken crags of sandstone, flung in ordered confusion along heath and bracken – an Exmoor in miniature – and as the path descends, the Frankby woods spreading in the vale to your right recall the pastoral beauty of Cheshire.'

Such words still hold true today.

Kitty's Flash, Thurstaston Common. A typical Thurstaston landscape: in the lower hollows, water collects, and here cotton-grass, with its fleecy flower heads that once were used to stuff pillows and eiderdowns, grows in profusion. In these damper areas, too, grows cross-leaved heather, one of the three heathers on the Common. On the higher, drier parts grow ling and bell heather, together with the low-growing and late-flowering western gorse.

OPPOSITE
'Sally's Cottage', also known as 'Shore Cottage', 'White Cottage' and the 'Customs Cottages', on the beach at Thurstaston below the cliffs of Wirral Country Park. Originally cottages for customs officers patrolling the Dee coast for smugglers, in more recent times this was the home of a local character, Sally McCrae. We get a fine glimpse of this lady from the jottings of a sailing family who found themselves washed ashore here in the 1940s: 'When you wade ashore from the sea and come to a cottage that has for 300 years been a landmark for seafarers, you touch living history. It still is a friendly guide to those who use the river, to fishermen threading their way through unbuoyed swatchways. There Miss McCrae, aged 83, had lived since the year I was born. She would have passed for a lively 60 any day, but especially on Saturdays when she donned her best hat and set out to climb the steep cliff path, walking another mile uphill to catch her bus for a day in Birkenhead.'

ABOVE
Irby Hall, Irby: one of Wirral's finest old halls. With views across to the Welsh hills, and close to the Dee, this ancient village ('the home of the Irish') was often under threat of invasion from the Welsh; hence the moat around the old hall.

RIGHT
The Irby Mill, a popular Irby inn, and formerly adjacent to a well-loved landmark of olden times, the windmill that was demolished 100 years ago.

Wirral Country Park

I first encountered what was to become Britain's first country park back in 1969, before much had happened to convert the old railway route into a tourist attraction. It was a dull, overcast day in March, with a frisky westerly wind rustling the previous autumn's leaves around our ankles. 'On the map, this old track looked quite promising: it ran alongside the Dee for much of its course, and passed quite near some of our favourite Wirral villages. If we got fed up, or wet, we could always hop on a bus home. In the event we did get tired; we got wet too: but fed-up? No! Perhaps it was the excitement of exploring the unknown; or the hazards of negotiating old railway ironmongery lying hidden in waist-high undergrowth. But that day was something special – the beginning of an attachment with part of our heritage which today, perhaps, we take rather for granted.'

Forty years on, the Wirral Way and its adjacent landscape are still an important part of my life. Scarcely a day goes by when I'm not touching it in some way in my Wirral wayfarings. I still love it – more than ever, perhaps. It's a place that always has something new to surprise me with – in its wildlife, its scenery; even its skyscapes vary from season to season, from day to day, from hour to hour. And this patch above the cliffs at Thurstaston is surely the best. Here, land, sea and sky combine with the elements of wind and weather to, on some days, blow me back into Wirral with their energy; on other days to stroke me with their warmth and gentleness. And always, the romance of bygone tracks and trains to fire the imagination . . .

DEESIDE REFLECTIONS

LEFT
Springtime on a section of the Wirral Way.

BELOW
Stone on the meadows above the Dee, Wirral Country Park, Thurstaston, commemorating the opening of the Park in 1973. The railway that was the forerunner of Wirral Country Park was completed from Hooton to West Kirby in 1886. In the early years the line prospered, linking the small agricultural communities of west Wirral with Chester, Birkenhead and Liverpool, and bringing townspeople to the seaside resorts on 'cheap day excursions'. Eventually, though, with the growing popularity of the car, the line suffered and the last passenger train ran on 17 September 1956. The hardware was removed in 1965, leaving only the grass and brambles to creep across the chippings.

The Wirral Green Belt Council was among the first to see the potential of the course of the former railway line, and in 1969 Cheshire County Council, backed by the Countryside Commission, started work on converting the track. Back in 1982 I wrote:

'To the walker today, the railway's past is continually present. The chippings underfoot form a constant reminder of the route's original purpose.

Hidden in the undergrowth at the side of the path, the diligent searcher will find gradient posts; old platforms and sidings now serve as picnic areas and car parks; while almost every section has its smoke-blackened bridge under which the rain-drenched walker can shelter. And it is rumoured that in the dead of night the whistles of long-forgotten trains echo through the cuttings, and red tail-lamps disappear into the darkness.'

PAGES 126–127
Thurstaston Visitor Centre at Wirral Country Park.

Heswall and Gayton

'What makes a happy communal life? Is it thriving trade, adequate open spaces, good drains, powerful parsons and brightly lit hostelries? All of these – which, if we may say so, Heswall possesses – make their contribution. Yet the vital element, of course, is people who, about their daily path, set the tenor of a local atmosphere and make it grave or gay, purposeful or indolent. Life is richer when people meet and mix together in understanding and can share their interests at work or play.

In a short walk in Heswall, one may move from the bustle of the busy streets, through quiet, homely roads, to the open country and the wide spaces where the sea-winds blow. One may choose the warm comradeship of well-lit roads with nearby shops, or the quieter homestead amid the fields, with a view of the river and the mountains beyond. Looking back to a rich past, and onwards to a promising future, the Heswall-of-the-Present is a rewarding place to know.'

(*Heswall and Gayton Guide*, 1958)

BELOW
The Devon Doorway at Gayton, a well-known and much-loved landmark for people coming into this part of Wirral from Chester along the high road.

OPPOSITE
The Black Horse Inn, Lower Heswall.

Heswall Parish Church, dedicated to St Peter, stands on a fine site in the Lower Village with wide-ranging views westwards over the Dee to the Welsh hills. The oldest part is the fourteenth-century tower, the rest of the building having been rebuilt in 1739 and again in 1879 after a great thunderbolt burst over it during Evensong, killing the organist and the boy who was blowing the bellows. Although seemingly far removed from the mainstream of national and international affairs, the church has played its part in the history of England, for on the

occasion of Queen Caroline's triumphant return to England in 1820 against the wishes of her husband, KIng George IV, 'the bells of Heswall church were rung out in defiance of all authority, and beacons blazed by the rocky lych-gate all through the night'. Caroline, it seems, had a special place in the hearts of the people of Heswall.

The church has many fine memorials and inscriptions, none so fine, though, as that to Katherine Glegg (wife of Edward Glegg of Gayton). This amazing lady, who was married in 1650 and died in 1666, aged 40, bore 13 sons and 2

daughters in her 16 years of married life! Despite the trials and tribulations of bringing into the world all those children, the memorial tells us that Katherine was still 'to all wives a president of chastity; to all matrons an example of gravity; to all persons a pattern of piety; she was most loving to her husband, careful with her children, respectful to her relations and equals, courteous to her inferiors, charitable to the poor, true-hearted to her friends, kind to her servants, and a cordial lover of all pious ministers and good persons'.

'Heswall 40 years ago was a picturesque village on the banks of the Dee, and the hills were unenclosed land over which the visitor could roam at his sweet will amidst a wealth of heather and gorse, and the picturesque cottages situated on the sides of its steep hills ended in the village. Now it is served by two systems of railways and has become a residential quarter for people engaged in business in Liverpool, Birkenhead and Chester. Many excellent modern and picturesque houses have been built, for it is high ground standing between two rivers, whose wide estuaries ensure it a healthful situation, one of the summits rising to 300 feet above sea level. The pleasant walk over the fields, through the churchyard to the shore, which bathers used to follow in the early 1870s, is disused, and a Macadam road runs down to the shore, by which some houses have been built; and a field on the brink of the shore now holds swing-boats. But little need be seen of the swing-boats, and Heswall still wears an air of rurality, for cottages in the village remain with thatched roofs, which are neat and tidily kept, while the swallows congregate there as of yore.'

(Harold Young, *A Perambulation of the Hundred of Wirral*, 1909)

The Dee Marshes, Lower Heswall

'The Dee is an estuary of many moods. The tranquility of a June day when the summer tide creeps over the sun-baked sands with scarcely a ripple and the Welsh mountains lie hidden beneath the soft veil of a heat haze – can this be the same sea that, in autumn, floods the estuary with a carpet of angry grey water, whipped to foam by a west wind, breaking in showers of spray over my bird island? In October gales, the tide rushes up the gutters with force enough to create a miniature bore, and wind-blown ocean wanderers such as petrels and puffins are found within the confines of the estuary.

The scene changes to winter's icy grip: the mudbanks frozen between the tides and the flood forcing its way along gutters half choked with broken ice. For a picture of utter desolation, it would be hard to find a better setting than saltings in hard frost. The marsh grass is coated with white; the sky a leaden pall; only the sound of one's boots on the iron surface breaks the oppressive silence.'

(Guy Farrar, *Feathered Folk of an Estuary*, 1938)

Boats moored on the marsh, near Sheldrakes Restaurant.

Shelduck are frequently seen on the Dee Estuary. Shown here is a drake shaking off excess water after bathing.

Sheldrakes Restaurant, on the edge of the marshes, Heswall.

The Old Haven

Old houses grey with wind and sun so placed
Along the airy margins of the Dee,
That each in turn looks out across the waste
Of drifting sand and shallow to the sea.

Old boats low-moored upon the channel's edge,
Asleep and dreaming of tomorrow's tide;
A mist of nets along the paling-ledge,
A spread of sail-cloth that the sun has dried.

A group of fisherfolk with southern eyes,
And accents borrowed from a bygone day,
The scream of seagulls and the far-off cries
Of wildfowl flying home from Hilbry way:

The is Old Haven and the place I love;
I love the sea-wall that its tides have broke,
The sandy shallows and the gulls above,
The houses, boats and nets and fisherfolk.

These redolent lines are by one of Heswall's
sons, John Pride, born in Lancashire in 1877
but who eventually made Lower Heswall his
home. Pride was a bohemian, a colourful
character in every sense of the word, and this
zest for living found expression through his
fondest mediums – poetry and art. In words
and in sketches he recorded both his
philosophical thoughts about life and death,
and his appreciation of the lovely Wirral
countryside in which he spent so much time.

Parkgate and Neston

'All on one side – like Parkgate' runs the old Cheshire saying, signifying the raw end of a deal. And raw deals were to be had in plenty in old Parkgate, particularly for those unfortunate enough to be left waiting for wind and tide to be right for their vessel to leave for Ireland! Picture the scene about 1750, wintertime: a nor-westerly gale has been blowing steadily for days. Travellers from the south, fearing Welsh terrors in the mountain passes en route for Holyhead, have opted to sail from Parkgate instead. The Irish-bound vessels lie straining at anchor out in the Dee, tossed and torn by the merciless winds blowing in from the Irish Sea.

On shore the passengers, among them perhaps Dean Swift or John Wesley, pass the long hours, snug and well entertained in the cosy Wirral inns, but spending both time and money which could no doubt be better used elsewhere. Not that the Parkgate innkeepers worry too much about that!

At last the skies clear, the seas subside, the wind drops a little and comes round from the south; and suddenly all is hustle and bustle on the quayside. The Irish boat will leave at noon!

Such times seem so remote now, with one-sided Parkgate facing westwards across the greensward of marshes which seem as immeasurable as the sea itself: a rushy carpet unfurling to the very foothills of Wales. Can this be the same place to which folk flocked from near and far to delight in the resort's facilities for the newly found pastime of sea bathing? Fine golden sands, health-giving breezes and magnificent views lured those who could afford to idle away hours in this way. From all over the north and midlands they came, to sample Parkgate's delights. I wonder . . . what did the local fisher-folk, those who made a meagre living from the dangerous, swirling waters of the Dee, think of it all? Did they ignore it? Were they slightly envious? Or did they, perhaps, make a pretty penny or two themselves during these decades of plenty pouring into the place?

Today, the sea has gone, the travellers have gone, the sea-bathers have gone, the fisher-folk have gone. But every fine afternoon, winter and summer, brings nose-to-tail parking along the front. People walk from one end of the long Parade to the other to study the detail of the hotchpotch of old buildings along the front, to feel the fresh west wind blowing on their faces from across the desolate marsh, to capture that unique feeling that only Parkgate can give – a slightly surreal landscape of wide skies, marsh and hills; they come, too, to gaze across the marshes; to recapture

that sense of history that is written along this short mile of quayside. And in their mind's eye, what do they see? Ghosts of sailing ships leaving for Ireland? Bathing-machines with their occupants coyly splashing about in the water? Fishing boats returning, low in the water with their day's catch? All of these, perhaps . . . and yet none.

But let's not ignore the buildings, the old inns and entertainment houses which were so prominent in Parkgate's past, and whose histories are well documented in the little guide-books on sale in the local shops. Consider how welcoming this little cluster of houses and inns must have appeared to the sea-weary travellers approaching Parkgate 250 years ago after a long and hazardous sea voyage. Buy the famed Parkgate ice-cream, nibble the Parkgate shrimps, and – enjoy Parkgate as those travellers of old enjoyed Parkgate too!

RIGHT
The Boathouse Inn, the 'first and last' building on Parkgate's front, and a familiar landmark to local folk.

BELOW LEFT
A Barn Owl hunts across the marsh in the evening.

BELOW
'All on one side': Parkgate front seen from the marsh.

Neston Parish Church, dedicated to St Mary and St Helen, has foundations going back to the twelfth century, but inside is a fine collection of fragments of ancient sculptured stones, probably of Viking origin.

RIGHT
Neston Cross, heart of the town. Neston is old – there has probably been a settlement here since the ninth or tenth century – but its rise to become, for a time, the most populous place in Wirral, was due to the construction of the New Quay by the Dee in the middle of the sixteenth century. This development brought trade, commerce and custom to the town. Hotels and lodging-houses thrived and the place became an important market town and coaching station. Yet 100 years ago, a visitor described the place: 'Approaching it nowadays and passing up its long, straggling main street, one asks why it was ever classed as a town, so sleepy does it appear, and so absent is the scene of bustle and eagerness that is inseparable from a town, that one wonders why the little place should be served by two different lines of railway, and be the proud possessor of two railway stations, in different quarters.'

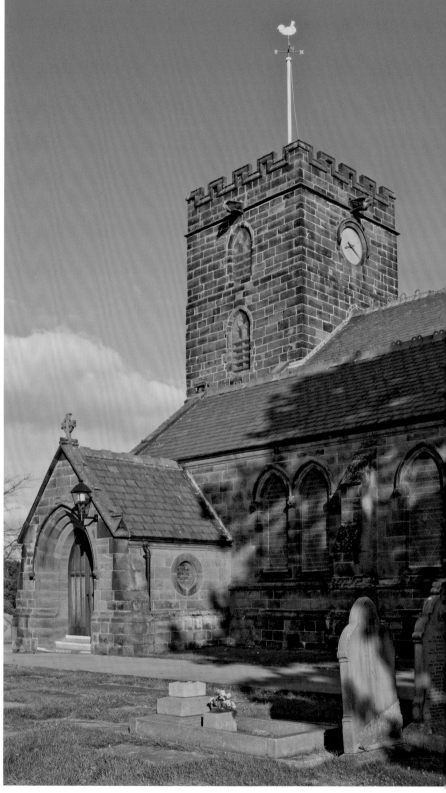

Neston mill, delightfully restored some years ago.

Detail from the mosaic on Neston's 'Millennium Project'.

Ness Gardens

South of Neston, on the road to Burton, is one of Wirral's gems: Ness Gardens. Here, on warm southwest-facing slopes above the Dee and with far-reaching views across the marshes to the Welsh hills, is a lovely place in which to idle away a few hours at any time of the year. In winter, the witch-hazels, snowdrops and winter aconite are among the first to shows signs of the coming spring; true spring blooms in a burst of colour with the rhododendrons and azaleas giving a wonderful display; the formal flower-beds and borders of high summer are a highlight of the gardens, as are the informal wildflower meadows looking across the Dee; and autumn brings the tints of the trees in their full glory.

Restoration and development work in recent years has made Ness Gardens one of the 'must-visit' places of the Wirral area – and a place to return to time and time again.

Burton

Burton churchyard on a summer's evening: swallows and house-martins skim low over the time-worn headstones; a weary rambler rests thankfully in the lush grass in the shade of the old square tower; children's voices echo from deep within the adjacent woods; and time itself seems to carry no meaning in the musky, dusky air of this ancient place. Burton slumbers on.

But it was not always so. Four hundred years ago the village boasted five licensed alehouses (there are none now!) scattered along the main street. These were busy days for Burton, with trading vessels anchoring in the shelter of the rocky headland down by the Dee, and goods of every description being brought ashore for conveyance to Chester. Small wonder then that the parish church is dedicated to St Nicholas, patron saint of both mariners and moneylenders. There were probably plenty of both in medieval Burton!

There are reminders of Burton's past in every nook and cranny of the village. The cottages perched high on the outcropping sandstone along the main street testify to antiquity; search out the birthplace and home of Bishop Wilson, one-time Bishop of the Isle of Man and benefactor to old Burton; consider the many building styles and materials used in the cottages; and admire the quiet beauty of the old-fashioned flower gardens.

The Dee is unseen, but not too distant from Burton village. The river wends a wayward course beyond the extensive marsh – several thousand acres managed by the RSPB. Here, now high and dry but once visited twice daily by the waters of the Irish Sea, stood the ancient hospital of Denwall. Founded in the Dark Ages 'for the poor applicants of Ireland and others', there is nothing left now but a few lumps and bumps in the fields down by the marsh.

From here we look back towards the village lying snugly beneath its tree-clad hill, peaceful, serene. I recall the words of another visitor to this place about the turn of the nineteenth century, and nod assent to his comments: 'Burton, ever beautiful, is a place to linger in towards evening. Except the softened ring of the anvil towards the end of the village, not a sound comes from the shaded street. Beyond the marshes there is no murmur from the sleeping tide. The complaining note of the woodquest dies in the leafy thickness. Twilight has found you a haunt of ancient peace.'

PREVIOUS PAGE
The Parish Church of St Nicholas, Burton. Built in 1721, this is the third church on this site. As well as being patron saint of pawnbrokers, St Nicholas is also patron saint of mariners – very fitting for this one-time maritime place.

LEFT
Burton Manor, one of the finest buildings in the village. Once the home of the Gladstones and the Congreves, the house has more recently been an educational study and conference centre. A team of volunteers has also started work on restoring parts of the grounds.

OPPOSITE, TOP
'Barn End' cottage, Burton village.

OPPOSITE, BOTTOM
'Bishop Wilson's Cottage', Burton village. Thomas Wilson was born in this cottage in 1663. At the age of 34 he became Bishop of Sodor and Man, a post which he held until his death at 93. The Manx bishopric was very poorly paid, yet he constantly refused offers of more rewarding sees in England and Ireland. It was once said that 'no collector of books felt quite happy unless he possessed a large paper copy of Bishop Wilson's edition of the Bible'. It is said that the main beam of the cottage is a ship's mast, probably retrieved from a wreck by the Dee.

Puddington and Shotwick

'Shotwick Village only' declares the road-sign beside the busy Welsh Road, pointing down an inviting hedge-banked country lane which twists and turns through the lush pasture-lands of this southernmost extremity of Wirral. The lane ends at silent Shotwick, a rewarding surprise for those who take the trouble to seek it out – a cluster of old Cheshire cottages watched over by the solid-looking red sandstone church. You will find here no inn, no village store or post-office: only the TV aerials remind us that we are in the twenty-first century. What you *will* find, in the stones of the buildings and in the pattern of the surrounding countryside, is a record of the

past, a past which is one of the most colourful in the peninsula and which belies the peace and tranquility of this wonderful place.

A stroll past the church down the cobble-stoned lane sets the scene: during Roman times, perhaps even earlier, Cheshire salt was carried into Wales along this 'Saltesway', which was later used as the 'King's Highway' to lead 'the host of our Sovreign Lord the King in time of War unto Shotwick Ford'. Henry III and Edward I used this track and its ford over the Dee to lead their armies into Wales during the warring years of the thirteenth century; and despite the hazards of shifting sands, wayward channels

The Parish Church of Shotwick, St Michael's. This fine building looking across the old sea-lands of the Dee is well worth a visit to view the fine Norman doorway and three-decker pulpit, age-darkened box pews and many other fascinating features to be expected in a building of such antiquity (see the deep grooves in the porch where the Wirral archers sharpened their arrows). But what are mere words when describing such an ancient, holy building as this? Words alone cannot convey autumn sunlight filtering through coloured glass and tinting the rough-hewn stone walls; or the wooden box-pews dark with age; or the cold, grey stone floor trodden by centuries of worshippers' feet. Sitting alone in the church, one's mind seeks and searches for answers to questions: What kind of people worshipped here? And what role did the church play in Shotwick's history?

OPPOSITE
A corner of Puddington village.

and unpredictable tides, peacetime travellers preferred this to the more circuitous route into Wales.

But this tale of tides, shifting sands and channels seems far removed from the scene before us today – a far-reaching, flat landscape of green fields backed by the hills of Wales. Can this Shotwick be the same place that once boasted a harbour, a safe anchorage where merchant and warrior fleets lay at anchor? Yes, for Shotwick was long ago perched right on the coast-line of the Dee; only a field's-length from the church the clay cliffs were twice daily washed by the tide. The steep, grass-covered cliff-line remains today, stranded by thousands of acres of silted-up pasture land; and the old creek to the south of the church still conjures up images of boats at anchor. The waters of the Dee, alas, visit Shotwick's shores no more.

Stroll through this quiet village, admire the characteristic Cheshire cottages with their old-fashioned gardens; seek out the old

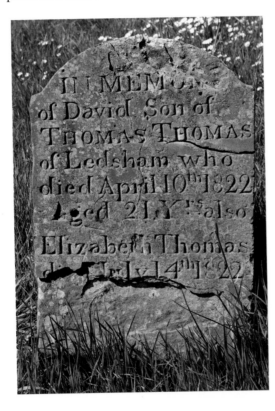

hall. Savour the peace and tranquility today, but in your imagination picture the scene from Shotwick's busy past: 'The great barons assembled here with their retinues, the street ringing to the tramp of armed men marching with warlike bustle, and in the mornings the famous Wirral archers at practice with their longbows'. Savour all this and be thankful that, despite the reminders of industrial Welsh Deeside in the far-off distance, Shotwick remains unique, untouched – and relatively silent.

LEFT, TOP
St Michael's churchyard is scattered with ancient, moss-covered tombstones, some with lovely old lettering.

LEFT, BOTTOM
Grooves in the porch may be from archers sharpening their arrows.

RIGHT
The churchyard cross and one of Shotwick's lovely old cottages.

The Wirral portion of a map of Cheshire by John Speede, 1611, with a corner of Chester inset top-right. The peninsula looks very different from the way it does today: the River Dee flows close to the Wirral shore, where now there is only marshland; the strange shape of Hilbre; the promontories at Neston and at Dove Point, Meols; and of course the different spellings of place-names.